Ben Carson versus Hillary Clinton

Presidential Election 2016

I0419813

Table of Contents

Taxes

Overview

Hillary Clinton would basically keep the same tax system in place while raising rates and removing deductions for people making $250,000 and higher. Ms. Clinton has also proposed a complex capital gains tax system that would raise rates on short term investments significantly and force investors to hold investments for up to six years to get the lowest rate. Clinton has also proposed more tax breaks for businesses that do profit sharing and for healthcare expenses for the "middle class". The bottom line is Hillary Clinton would keep the overall structure of our tax system with the IRS and make it more complex, with "the rich" shouldering more of the tax burden.

Ben Carson approaches taxation using the principle of "tithing" from the Bible. What he means by this is proportionality, so that everyone would pay the same *proportion* of their total income in taxes. Carson is basically in favor of an across the board flat tax. He has suggested a rate somewhere around 15%. So everyone would pay the same proportion. A person making $50,000 a year would pay $7,500, while a person earning $100,000 a year would pay $15,000. They pay the same proportion, or another way to look at it is the person making twice as much income pays twice as much tax. Ben Carson's plan would dramatically simplify and restructure our tax code and the IRS.

Capital Gains

Before we look at the proposals from the candidates, lets briefly review current law. Under current law, a long term gain is defined as one longer than a year and capital gains taxes are levied on a two-tiered structure. The tax rate is figured in two parts, a statutory rate and a surtax. For an investment held less than a year, the total tax rate is 43.4% which includes a 39.6% statutory rate and a 3.8% investment income surtax. If an investment is held a year or longer, the tax rate is much lower. In that case the total capital gains tax is 23.8%, including the 3.8% investment income surtax.

Hillary Clinton's Plan

- For investments held 1-2 years, there would be a 39.6% statutory tax rate.
- For investments held 2-3 years, there would be a 36% statutory tax rate.
- For investments held 4 years, there would be a 32% statutory tax rate.
- For investments held 5 years, there would be a 28% statutory tax rate.
- For investments held 6 years, there would be a 24% statutory tax rate.
- For investments held longer than 6 years there would be a 20% statutory tax rate.

One can see right away that a Hillary Clinton administration will be beloved by accountants and tax lawyers. On her website, she explains the rationale of this plan as encouraging long term investments instead of short term profits and planning for the future. Clinton is not proposing this system to increase government revenue, but rather to manipulate the behavior of people and corporations. The tax foundation claims it would even slightly decrease revenue.

Critics say Hillary Clinton's capital gains tax plan would be bad for the economy.

http://nypost.com/2015/08/01/hillary-clintons-tax-plan-would-be-devastating-critics/

Larry Kudlow, financial commentator at CNBC called her plan "inconceivably stupid".

http://limittaxes.org/wp-content/uploads/2015/08/Hillary%E2%80%99s-Tax-Reform-Throwback-Reveals-There-Is-Nothing-Progressive-About-Progressivism-_-The-Daily-Caller-20150804.pdf

Ben Carson's Plan

Ben Carson's ideas on taxes are consistent across the board and simple. His plan for capital gains taxes is a 15% flat tax. Carson claims that with a flat tax rate at about 15% it would be a revenue-neutral plan, in other words his tax system would bring in about the same amount of revenue as the current system. Again Carson sites his Biblical beliefs as a basis for the plan, the Bible says to "tithe" 10%. The proportion used for tithing in the Bible is the same regardless of whether you had a bumper crop or a bad year.

In his own words:

"We don't necessarily have to do 10% but it's the principle. He didn't say if your crops fail, don't give me any tithe or if you have a bumper crop, give me triple tithe. So there must be something inherently fair about proportionality. You make $10 billion, you put in a billion. You make $10 you put in one. Of course you've got to get rid of the loopholes. Some people say, 'Well that's not fair because it doesn't hurt the guy who made $10 billion as much as the guy who made 10.' Where does it say you've got to hurt the guy? He just put a billion dollars in the pot. We don't need to hurt him. It's that kind of thinking that has resulted in 602 banks in the Cayman Islands. That money needs to be back here building our infrastructure and creating jobs."

Since Carson made this comment he has come out in favor o the 15% rate.

Hillary Clinton on Income Taxes

Hillary Clinton has yet to propose a detailed income tax plan at the time of writing, but in the past she has stated she preferred the tax rates of the 1990s. When Bill Clinton left office, his administration had a top tax rate of 39.6% on $288,350 of income. Ms. Clinton has stated repeatedly that she would raise rates on those making more than $250,000 of income. So it appears that she would prefer a 39.6% income tax rate for those making $250,000 a year or higher.

Checking the inflation calculator maintained by the Bureau of Labor Statistics (see http://www.bls.gov/data/ inflation_calculator.htm), an income today of $250,000 has the same purchasing power as an income of $181,006 in the year 2000.

That means that Hillary Clintons proposal would be equivalent to a 39.6% income tax on people making $181,000 in 2000. In other words, her proposal imposes an income tax that would be much higher than it was in the 1990s when considering real purchasing power.

Ms. Clinton says she will reduce taxes for the middle class and working families, but as yet has provided no specifics.

Hillary Clinton plans to complicate the tax code by adding new deductions. She says she wants to invest in the "Caring Economy". Her proposals include:

- A 20% tax credit for households that can document spending $6,000 on elderly family members. She states this will give a household up to $1,200 in tax savings.
- A tax credit of up to $2,500 per student in a family attending college.
- End the carried interest loophole.
- Enact the "Buffet Rule".
- Reduce deductions available to "wealthy" tax payers.

Ben Carson on Income Taxes

Again, Ben Carson favors a 15% flat tax. Under Carson's plan at the time of writing, there would be no loopholes or deductions. In Carson's words:

"Every citizen of the US should be expected to contribute to its welfare, which requires a fair system of taxation. We currently do not have such a system, because our tax code is so complex that those with good tax attorneys or accountants can find numerous loopholes to avoid paying their fair share of taxes. Given our country's financial crisis, the creation of a new and fairer tax system is urgently needed. The cries of "tax the rich" in the face of such a hypocritical tax code is, frankly, quite laughable. I do not believe that the rich are unpatriotic because they take advantage of loopholes, but I think we as a nation are smart enough to come up with a system of taxation that eliminates the need for slick accountants and lawyers, and that allows everyone to contribute proportionately to the financial health of the nation--just as God designed for us in the concept of the tithe."

Death or Estate Tax

Hillary Clinton

While claiming to be in favor of the estate tax, Hillary Clinton has personally worked with her husband to create their own nontaxable estate. In the 2008 campaign she proposed keeping estate tax rates at levels they would be in 2009. She hasn't given a specific proposal in 2015 but has indicated she is in favor an estate tax on the wealthy. Personally however, she is gaming the system to avoid any estate taxes on her own assets (see http://www.bloomberg.com/news/articles/2014-06-17/wealthy-clintons-use-trusts-to-limit-estate-tax-they-back).

Ben Carson

Ben Carson says he would repeal the estate tax. In his view, you don't tax anything twice and the wealth that is left in an estate has already been taxed before the person became deceased.

Corporate Taxes

According to KPMG, the United States has the highest corporate tax rate in the world at 40% (see https://home.kpmg.com/xx/en/home/services/tax/tax-tools-and-resources/tax-rates-online/corporate-tax-rates-table.html). Some view high corporate tax rates as a factor in driving income overseas.

Hillary Clinton

Hillary Clinton has not released a specific corporate tax rate proposal, but she has called for eliminating deductions. She plans to "encourage" companies to share profits, offering a 15% tax break for companies that use profit sharing. From her website:

"Ensure more workers share in near-record corporate profits. Corporate profits are near record highs — but workers have not shared through rising wages. Profit sharing is linked to higher pay, benefits, and productivity. That's why Hillary's plan creates a 15 percent tax credit for companies that share profits with workers on top of wages and pay increases. "

Ben Carson

Ben Carson plans to drastically cut the US corporate tax rate from 40% down to a level of between 15-20%.

Summary

Under Hillary Clinton, taxes will go up on high earners. More deductions and rules will be added to the tax code making the current 70,000+ page tax code even more complicated. Middle class earners will possibly be able to get lower tax rates by taking advantage of available tax credits. Investment taxes will increase and get more complicated. In short Hillary Clinton's plan will be more of the same but more complicated, perhaps beloved by tax lawyers and accountants.

Ben Carson's plan will be simple with his principle of proportionality applied to all forms of income. Those favoring progressive taxation and income redistribution will not like Ben Carson's plan. The IRS would likely shrink under Carson, and tax lawyers and accountants would have to find other lines of work. Under Ben Carson, rates would be drastically lower across the board with deductions eliminated.

References

http://www.ontheissues.org/2016/
Ben_Carson_Tax_Reform.htm

http://www.breitbart.com/video/2015/11/09/carson-flat-tax-would-have-to-be-about-15-to-be-revenue-neutral/

https://www.hillaryclinton.com/issues/plan-raise-american-incomes/

http://www.latimes.com/nation/politics/la-na-hillary-clinton-taxes-20151123-story.html

http://taxfoundation.org/

http://www.bls.gov/data/inflation_calculator.htm

http://www.rfdtv.com/story/29845942/dr-ben-carson-on-taxes

http://www.cbsnews.com/news/after-touting-estate-tax-bill-and-hillary-clinton-seize-on-loopholes/

http://www.huffingtonpost.com/entry/ben-carson-tax-policy_5616a91be4b0e66ad4c6d9a0

Minimum Wage

With rising prices, declining job opportunities and fast food workers demanding a $15 an hour wage, the minimum wage is an issue (at least for the left). Liberals demand a "living wage" be paid for menial work. Where do the candidates stand?

Hillary Clinton

Hillary Clinton supports raising the minimum wage to $12 an hour. She has also stated she supports efforts by fast food workers to get a $15 an hour minimum wage.

Ben Carson

Ben Carson supports raising the minimum age and indexing it to inflation. However he has not given a specific value he supports for the minimum wage. Carson also suggests there should be a two-tiered minimum wage, with a lower rate for young people. He says this will allow young workers with no work experience to get more access to entry level jobs. Carson supports the view that increasing the minimum wage leads to job losses.

References

https://www.hillaryclinton.com/issues/plan-raise-american-incomes/

http://www.forbes.com/sites/timworstall/2015/09/21/ben-carsons-half-a-good-idea-on-the-minimum-wage/

Gun Rights

Hillary Clinton

Generally speaking, Ms. Clinton is pro-gun control. Hillary Clinton has posted several specific proposals on her website. These are summarized here:

- Hillary Clinton supports and assault weapons ban. On her website she states "Military-style assault weapons do not belong on our streets." Ms. Clinton fails to note that rifles available to the general public such as the AR-15 are not the same as assault weapons used by the military, although she implicitly acknowledges it by calling them "military-style" weapons.
- Hillary Clinton supports closing "loopholes" that allow the mentally ill to purchase guns, but doesn't say what those loopholes are.
- Hillary Clinton proposes making "straw purchasing" a crime. This is when a person knowingly buys a gun for someone else who is prohibited from purchasing guns by law.
- Expand ban on domestic abusers from purchasing guns. Currently a married person convicted of domestic violence cannot buy a gun. Hillary Clinton wants to extend this law to people in "dating relationships" and stalkers.
- Open gun manufacturers to law suits. Ms. Clinton proposes allowing people to sue gun manufacturers and dealers if a weapon made (or sold in the case of dealers) by the manufacturer is used in a violent crime.

- Revoke licenses of dealers found to be allowing straw man purchases and illegal trafficking of firearms. From her website she states "As president, she will provide funding to increase inspections and aggressively enforce current law by revoking the licenses of dealers that knowingly supply straw purchasers and traffickers."
- Require background checks at gun shows and for internet purchases. Of course Ms. Clinton doesn't acknowledge background checks are already required for internet purchases.
- Introducing "Comprehensive" background checks for all gun purchases. Its unclear what she means by this since background checks are already required.

Ben Carson

Ben Carson is unapologetically in favor of the second amendment. He is against gun registration and doesn't believe the second amendment should be infringed in any way. Several years ago Carson suggested that assault weapons should not be allowed in cities but he has recently backed away from that stance. Carson states one of the reasons for the second amendment is for the people to defend themselves against a tyrannical government.

Summary

Under Ben Carson, gun laws would continue as they are now. Under Hillary Clinton there would be bans on assault weapons, increased background checks, and the ability to sue gun manufacturers and dealers (assuming she could either get these through Congress or implement these changes by executive order).

Healthcare

With the passage of the Affordable Care Act commonly known as "Obamacare", management of our healthcare system is a central issue.

Hillary Clinton

Many voters will remember that Hillary Clinton was put in charge of the first attempt in recent years by Democrats to bring government run healthcare for all to the United States. That effort failed because of the political atmosphere of the time. Hillary Clinton has somewhat backed off but her views remain basically the same. On her website she declares "Affordable healthcare is a basic human right". Notice this is different from saying "healthcare is a basic human right".

Hillary Clinton has posted a detailed position paper on healthcare on her website. A few highlights:

- Hillary Clinton will keep Obamacare in place and fight any Republican effort to repeal it.
- She supports lowering copays and deductables, but does not give any specifics on what she would lower them too or how these reductions would be paid for.
- Price controls on prescription drugs. Ms. Clinton does not address how this would impact pharmaceutical research.
- Increase rural health clinics.
- Increased federal support for "telehealth" remote healthcare consultations, presumably for those living in rural areas.
- Ensure women have access to "reproductive healthcare".
- Completely fund Planned Parenthood.
- Supports a woman's right to abortion.

Ben Carson

Ben Carson is against Obamacare, and would repeal it. Ideas that he has supported include:

- Creation of Health Savings Accounts for each citizen. These would be created at birth. Contributions to Health Savings Accounts would be pre-tax and the HSA could be passed on to other family members upon death.
- Carson has suggested diverting money from Medicare and Medicaid to help fund Health Savings Accounts for the poor. He has proposed providing up to $5,000 per year for 80 million Americans to put in their HSAs. In some cases he has proposed funding everyones HSA with $2,000.
- People would have the option of purchasing insurance for catastrophic health events. He would also make enrolling in Medicaid and Medicare optional over time. This would also be for catastrophic coverage. The HSA would be the primary method of paying for healthcare under his plan.
- Ben Carson states he is 100% pro-life, but doesn't explicitly say if he would attempt to ban abortion or not.
- Carson has noted the problems created for businesses by Obamacare and believes its a drag on the economy.
- Stiff penalties for Medical Fraud.
- He has proposed regulating insurance companies as non-profits.

Summary and References

Hillary Clinton will keep Obamacare in place, and possibly expand on it. Ms. Clinton also favors price controls on pharmaceuticals. Carson will repeal Obamacare and institute Health Savings Accounts and possibly some other changes.

https://www.hillaryclinton.com/issues/health-care/

https://www.bostonglobe.com/business/2015/09/22/clinton-plan-control-prescription-drug-prices-push-down-biotech-shares-for-second-day/5Ol1H4BZgQicoWr7MBFfwM/story.html

http://www.ontheissues.org/2016/Ben_Carson_Health_Care.htm

https://www.washingtonpost.com/posteverything/wp/2015/10/29/ben-carsons-health-care-prescription-is-no-cure-for-what-ails-americans/ (disclosure - Ezekiel Emmanuel helped craft "Obamacare").

Social Security

Hillary Clinton

Ms. Clinton follows the standard Democratic party line of defending social security and medicare as is. Specific points on social security from her policy papers:

- No privatization of social security accounts.
- No change in cost of living adjustments.
- She will not raise the retirement age.
- Expand social security benefits for those that took time off from working for childcare. This seems to amount to a welfare handout for those who took time off from work so were not paying into the social security system.
- Raise the cap on income for which social security tax is paid, but she does not give a specific number.
- Preserve medicare and fight any Republican attempt to phase it out or privatize it.
- Have medicare negotiate lower drug prices.

Ben Carson

- Gradually raise the retirement age. This would only be done for those under the age of 55.
- Forbid the government from using social security revenue for other purposes.
- Allow interest rates to rise to encourage savings so people would not be as dependent on social security in retirement.
- Allow people that don't need social security to opt-out.

Climate Change/Energy

Hillary Clinton

When it comes to climate change Hillary Clinton is a true believer. She says she wants to make the United States the "clean energy superpower of the 21st century". Her proposals include the following:

- Power every home in America with "renewable" wind and solar energy by 2026.
- She claims to be "just a grandmother with two eyes and a brain" but she knows climate change will have a large impact on her daughter and grand-daughter. She says future generations will ask how we were so irresponsible if nothing is done about climate change.
- She says climate science is "settled" and urgent action is needed.
- She claims renewable energy will prevent 70,000 asthma attacks and 3,000 premature deaths per year.
- She claims the renewable energy industry has created 50,000 jobs and driven $35 billion of investment.
- On her first day in office she will set a goal of installing a half billion solar panels by the end of her first term.
- She claims the electrical grid will be more reliable and resilient.

Ben Carson

When it comes to climate change and energy, Ben Carson is practically the complete opposite of Hillary Clinton:

- Carson believes climate change is natural and will always occur, calling it an "irrelevant" debate.

- Carson believes in general environmental protection that is not based on the concept of climate change.
- He supports complete petroleum independence for the United States for political reasons. Carson would like to end our dependence on middle eastern states like Saudi Arabia to meet our energy needs.
- Carson believes we should utilize our own oil and natural gas resources, he supports responsible fracking and offshore drilling.
- Although climate change is not a central concern, Mr. Carson does support rapid development of renewable energy sources. Unlike Ms. Clinton he has not provided specific goals for the number of solar panels.

References

https://www.hillaryclinton.com/issues/climate/

http://www.ontheissues.org/2016/Ben_Carson_Energy_+_Oil.htm

Foreign Policy

With the rise of ISIS and a terrorist attack in Paris late in 2015, fighting terrorism and foreign policy figure to be major issues in the upcoming Presidential campaign. Here is where our two candidates stand on the issues. Having been Secretary of State, its not too surprising that Hillary Clinton has very detailed positions laid out on foreign policy. On her website she claims she believes in "free markets" throughout the world which seems to contradict her economic policy ideas at home.

Hillary Clinton

Much of the policy positions described on Hillary's website amount to hand waving, but she does take some definite positions and they often read as right of center. Hillary Clinton recognizes major threats and challenges to US National security, focusing on ISIS, China, and Iran getting a nuclear weapon. Her proposals, however, sound vague. For example, to defeat ISIS she says

"We will confront and defeat them in a way that builds greater stability across the region"

In recent speeches, Clinton has adopted a more assertive tone than her former boss Barak Obama, saying

"Our goal is not to deter or contain ISIS, but to defeat and destroy ISIS."

A few Hillary Clinton highlights in regard to ISIS:

- Hillary Clinton will not involve US ground troops in a war to fight ISIS, however she is open to expanding the commitment of US Special Operations forces in the region, from the 50 sent by Obama.
- She proposes building up the Iraqi military.
- She proposes to bring back stability to Libya and Yemen.
- Ms. Clinton has called upon Congress to approve a new authorization for the use of military force against ISIS.
- Overthrowing Assad is not the top priority in Syria. However she supports the Obama contention that there should be a "political solution" to the war in Syria that would force Assad out.
- She says the Russian's have a role to play but that Assad must go, something that Putin seems unlikely to agree with.
- Convince Turkey to stop bombing Kurdish groups.
- More airstrikes are needed. She calls not only for more airstrikes with more planes but also a broadening of targets. But she emphasizes that this should be a *coalition* operation, not an American one, and that it must be combined with a ground war (not conducted by the United States) to take back territory from ISIS on the ground.
- Clinton wants to go after terrorist financing from Saudi Arabia and Qatar, and proposes going after online recruitment and travel activities by westerners going to Syria to join ISIS.
- Clinton is committed to the survivability of Iraq, but with an inclusive government that brings the Sunni's into the fold.
- Hillary is in favor of a no-fly zone in Syria with Russian cooperation. However Russia has rejected the idea.
- Supports taking in refugees from Syria into the United States.
- Vaguely supports a commitment to Democracy and security in Afghanistan.

Next we turn to Hillary Clinton's views on Iran. Perhaps the most important thing to note is Ms. Clinton supports the Iran Nuclear Agreement Obama has put in place. She takes a harder line against Iran than Obama does at least in rhetoric, saying she will "distrust but verify" to borrow a line from Ronald Reagan, and that she will aggressively confront Iran's "unacceptable behavior" in the Middle East. Hillary's reputation as a Democrat Hawk among liberals comes through when reading her positions in regard to Iran, other than accepting the nuclear deal. For example:

- She proposes expanding the US military presence in the Persian Gulf region.
- Clinton goes against the liberal grain by claiming a firm commitment to Israel's security. Her pro-Israel stance includes supporting the sale to Israel of missile defense systems and advanced fighter aircraft. She also proposes she will continue intelligence sharing with Israel and will help them with tunnel and smuggling defenses. She sounds a lot more openly pro-Israel than Barak Obama.
- Clinton also proposes an active stance against Hezbollah and Hamas. Part of her proposal is to "build a coalition" to stand against these terrorist groups.
- She proposes possible sanctions against Iran if they continue sending weapons to "bad actors" such as North Korea and Syria, and possible human rights sanctions for Iran's abuses at home.

On Putin, Clinton claims she will go "toe to toe" with him and notes that she's done it before. She claims Putin pursues an outdated form of foreign policy that amounts to a "zero sum game". However much of what she says about Putin and Russia is vague, she says the United States must show "strength and patience".

In regard to China, Clinton's skill at bloviating is often on display. She spoke about China when describing Obama's failed "rebalance" strategy that was based on three elements:

"We are practicing robust regional engagement in the Asia-Pacific, we are working to build trust between China and the United States, and we are committed to expanding economic, political, and security cooperation wherever possible."

Sounds vague.

Clinton also claims "climate change" is a national security issue. On her website she writes:

"Climate change is not just a moral and economic issue, it is a defining national security challenge of our time. Safeguarding our country from rising sea levels and extreme weather requires domestic action and intensive global engagement. America must lead this effort, not back away from a threat to our security or an opportunity for our economy." (boldness added).

Clinton also identifies infectious disease as a national security threat. Again, identifying "climate change" as the root cause or at least as increasing the risk.

Ben Carson

CARSON ON ISRAEL

Ben Carson believes that due to the continued dependence of the United States on energy sources from the Middle East, that energy independence is a national security issue. Carson believes that energy independence will make the United States more secure as well as giving the United States more leverage with countries like Saudi Arabia. During one of the Presidential debates Carson claimed that he had suggested to GW Bush that if the US was not dependent on Saudi Arabia for oil supplies, that the US could pressure Saudi Arabia into turning over Bin Laden.

Carson is unwavering in his support for Israel. However he doesn't provide specifics, only general direction. Carson has stated Israel would not have to wonder about the support of the United States if he were President, saying that the United States would have Israel's back. Carson has stated that he could support a "two state solution" for Israel and the Palestinians provided that the Palestinian state was not close to urban Israeli centers.

He recently wrote

"Looking to the future, while remaining mindful of the past, I believe that it is in America's national security interests to deepen our commitment to Israel. If elected president in November 2016, I will explore every opportunity to strengthen ties between our two nations and to ensure that Israel always has the tools it needs to protect herself and our shared interests."

CARSON ON GUANTANAMO BAY

Carson is in favor of keeping Guantanamo bay open. He says the facility should be used for captured terrorists who would be tried by military commission.

CARSON ON IRAN
When it comes to Iran, Ben Carson is completely against the Iran Nuclear Deal signed by the Obama administration. Carson believes sanctions on Iran should not be lifted until their nuclear program is completely dismantled. According to Carson there should be anywhere-anytime inspections of Iranian facilities and the international community should keep the pressure on with harsh sanctions until Iran ends its nuclear program. Carson is also against aspects of the deal that allow Iran to sell weapons systems and ballistic missiles. Carson says he would require Iran's uranium stockpiles to be eliminated.

CARSON ON ISIS

Carson's general approach to dealing with the Islamic State is either fight them over there, or fight them later over here. Carson says ISIS is still in their development stage and we need to destroy them now. He asserts that if ISIS is allowed to grow we risk getting into a fight for our lives.

- Open to putting American troops on the ground to fight ISIS.
- Establish a no-fly zone along the Turkish border.
- The US should wage an informational and ideological war with ISIS to counter their message and propaganda.
- American troops should be able to fight without one hand tied behind their back with constraints on operations due to political correctness. Carson has stated that he would send flyers out to people telling them they had 72 hours to get out and then the region would be destroyed.
- The military should not be micromanaged. Soldiers will not be prosecuted for actions taken in warfare.
- Go after financial support of ISIS.
- The United States should commit immediately while ISIS is in its infant stage.
- Carson has suggested driving ISIS out of Iraq and push them entirely into Syria.
- The United States should directly support the Kurds.

CARSON ON PUTIN/RUSSIA

Ben Carson believes that the United States must respond aggressively to actions by Vladimir Putin. Dr. Carson sees Putin as a threat not only in the Ukraine but also in Syria and the Baltic region. He proposes giving Ukraine offensive weapons to help them in their fight against Russian seperatists. He also proposes putting a missile defense system in Eastern Europe.

CARSON ON CHINA

Carson identifies China as the most significant long term strategic challenge to the United States. He proposes the following:

- Re-establish a U.S. military presence in the Philippines.
- Aggressively sail ships through disputed waters and fly aircraft over disputed areas of the South China Sea claimed by China.
- Deploy the US Marines to Australia.
- Allow Japan to take on a combat mission in collective security in the region.
- Encourage security cooperation among powers in the region including Australia, Vietnam, the Philippines, Taiwan, South Korea, India and Japan.
- Retaliate if China engages in cyber-warfare.

http://www.cnn.com/2015/11/19/politics/hillary-clinton-isis-speech/

http://time.com/4120295/hillary-clinton-foreign-policy-isis/

http://www.huffingtonpost.com/entry/hillary-clinton-syria-russia_5614695de4b0fad1591a0574

http://www.jpost.com/Opinion/Never-Again-means-standing-with-Israel-423919

http://www.nbcnews.com/politics/2016-election/carson-slams-hypocrisy-his-doubters-foreign-policy-n468096
http://thehill.com/opinion/op-ed/253928-ben-carson-obama-needs-new-ideas-to-blunt-isis

http://nationalinterest.org/feature/how-compete-china-13925

http://www.cnn.com/2015/11/01/politics/ben-carson-syria-putin/

Immigration

Hillary Clinton apologized for saying "illegal immigrant". From that fact alone we can imagine there will be differences between her and the Republican candidates.

Hillary Clinton

- Ms. Clinton favors so-called "comprehensive immigration reform".
- Ms. Clinton favors a "path to citizenship" for illegal immigrants living inside the United States.
- Hillary Clinton will allow illegal immigrants to buy health insurance on the Obamacare exchanges. This means that tax payers would be subsidizing health insurance payments for low income illegal immigrants.
- If illegal immigrants arrive at the border as a family, Hillary supports "supervised release" of the family rather than detention.
- Hillary would end privatization of immigration detention centers and only have the government run them directly.
- She proposes only detaining and deporting those illegal immigrants that pose a risk of violent crime.
- Hillary would support all of Obama's executive actions related to immigration, and has suggested she would expand on them, using executive actions if necessary.
- Hillary favors "technology" and more personnel at the border rather than a border fence. In a recent comment she said ""I don't care how tall the wall is or how big the door is, that is never going to happen. And I think that's an unnecessarily provocative thing to say."

- Clinton has voiced support for aid to Mexico and Central American countries with the idea that development and increased security down there will reduce immigration to the United States.
- Hillary Clinton is in favor of taking in Syrian refugees.

Ben Carson

- Ben Carson supports "sealing" the border. He has a goal of sealing the southern border within the first year of his administration.
- As part of sealing the border Carson supports fencing where it will work, drones, electronic surveillance and border patrol workers.
- Carson has expressed support for a guest worker program in the agricultural sector. To qualify the applicant could not have a criminal record.
- Later Carson expressed support for a more general guest worker type program. He would give immigrants six months to register. They would not get citizenship or the right to vote.
- Carson is against a Trump style roundup of illegal immigrants - for practical reasons. He has said if someone can explain how to do it he would be wiling to listen.
- Carson states that a pathway to citizenship is unfair to current and past immigrants.
- After the Paris shootings Carson suggested the U.S. should maintain a database of all immigrants, but he was opposed to making a database singling out Muslim immigrants.
- Ben Carson is opposed to taking in Syrian refugees.

http://www.latintimes.com/hillary-clinton-bragging-about-building-border-wall-keeping-out-illegal-immigrants-352631
https://www.hillaryclinton.com/issues/immigration-reform/

http://www.ontheissues.org/2016/Ben_Carson_Immigration.htm

http://www.nationalreview.com/corner/ben-carson-immigration-plan-ian-tuttle

General Economic Issues

Hillary Clinton

Let's begin by looking at Hillary's claimed support for small businesses. A great deal of Hillary's campaign publications are simplistic bullet points without much detail with feel good phrases without further detail such as "Expand employment opportunities".

When it comes to small business, Hillary claims she will "cut red tape at all levels of government". She also notes the time and expense required for small business to do their taxes. Without saying how, she says she will "simplify tax filing" and provide "targeted tax relief" without saying what that would be.

Also without providing details, she claims she will help small business "tap new markets". Here she says:

"Some American businesses — like Etsy and eBay — are already doing this through innovative new platforms that let them sell anywhere in America and the world. Hillary will encourage this kind of innovation."

A lot of hot air without actually saying anything. In a similar vein she says she will reduce the burdens on small banks, and in turn this will open up more loans for small businesses, so she says.

A central theme for Clinton is the standard Democrat party claims that they will improve the economy with "investments" in infrastructure, clean energy, and scientific research.

Her bullet points for strong economic growth are the following (I leave it to the reader to determine whether or not these actions will actually contribute to economic growth):

• Expand employment opportunities (doesn't say how)
• Provide tax relief for the middle class and small business (doesn't say how)
• Enact comprehensive immigration reform
• Fund scientific and medical research
• Breakdown barriers for entering the workforce, especially for women (what does this even mean?)
• Expand job training
• Increase affordability of college

In addition Hillary Clinton offers these items to in her view, help the economy with "fair growth":

• Support for unions and collective bargaining
• Make the wealthy pay their "fair share" of taxes
• Invest in students and teachers
• Provide pathways into the middle class (says nothing about how this would be accomplished)
• Raise the minimum wage
• Encourage profit sharing by corporations
• Universal pre-school for 4 year olds
• Support Dodd-Frank and "go further" but doesn't provide specifics
• Strengthen Obamacare
• Expand overtime rules to millions of new workers

Ben Carson

Ben Carson has said "Most powerful stimulus to economic activity: knowledge that you can acquire things & these things will not be confiscated by the government."

We have already seen one aspect of Ben Carson's approach to the economy with a flat tax. Some of Ben Carson's ideas for the economy:

- A flat 15% tax on businesses and flat 15% tax on individuals
- Reduce government waste and fraud
- Supports a two tiered minimum wage, with a different rate for younger workers, but has voiced support for raising the minimum wage.
- Supports deregulation
- Believes the EPA hinders competitiveness of American companies
- Create job-friendly regulations and tax code
- Supports free markets
- Reduce welfare spending
- Carson believes the huge Federal debt is a major threat to the health of the economy.
- Has noted that very low interest rates impair the ability of people to build up personal savings.

In contrast to Hillary Clinton's blind support of unions Carson has said:

"In the early days unions brought about the kind of collective bargaining that resulted in fair wages and reasonable working conditions. With time, many of the union bosses began to concern themselves with power and influence. By threatening strikes to further their causes, they were able to exact excessive wages and benefits from companies such as General Motors, Ford and Chrysler, in the long run crippling these companies and rendering them noncompetitive. Essentially they were strangling the goose that laid the golden egg."

From his book:
America the Beautiful: What Makes This Country Great – Ben Carson, M.D. with Candy Carson, Zondervan, 2012

https://www.hillaryclinton.com/issues/plan-raise-american-incomes/

http://www.marketplace.org/2015/11/17/elections/full-interview-dr-ben-carson-economy

http://www.newsmax.com/NewsmaxTv/obama-wages-workers-employment/2014/01/31/id/550274#ixzz2vuGrRhWl

Government Debt

At the time of writing the Federal government has amassed more than $18 Trillion in debt. About half of this was during Obama's term in office. Net interest on the debt already costs the federal government about $224 billion annually. The debt drains money that might have been invested in private enterprise and poses a threat to economic security. A rise in interest rates could lead to the federal government having to spend catastrophic amounts on paying net interest on the debt. Where do the candidates stand on dealing with the national debt?

Hillary Clinton

If the national debt is a major concern for Hillary Clinton, you'd be hard pressed to find any evidence of this. On her issues page for her campaign its not even listed. Under economy its not listed either. In the past, she has claimed support for a balanced budget and suggested she was against tax cuts that would add to the debt. In 2000 she was suggesting using the supposed surplus to pay down the national debt.

In 2010 she said this about the national debt:

"It undermines our capacity to act in our own interest, and it does constrain us where constraint may be undesirable. And it also sends a message of weakness internationally. It is very troubling to me that we are losing the ability not only to chart our own destiny, but to have the leverage that comes from having this enormously effective economic engine that has powered American values and interests over so many years. So I don't think we have a choice – it is a question of how we decide to deal with this debt and deficit…. There is no free lunch, and we cannot pretend that there is without doing grave harm to our country and our future generations."

Before serving in the Obama administration, Hillary appears to have referred to the budget surplus that occurred under her husbands administration frequently. In this campaign, perhaps because she has tilted to the left on domestic issues, she hasn't said much about it. In fact she's proposing some crazy give aways like this one:

"I like the idea of giving every baby born in America a $5,000 account that will grow over time, so that when that young person turns 18 if they [sic] have finished high school they will be able to access it to go to college or maybe they will be able to make that downpayment on their first home." She added that "we want to make an investment in America's young people."

Perhaps Clinton will argue that the wealthy can take care of the debt by paying "their fair share" and/or the economy will grow us out of the debt.

Ben Carson

In contrast to Ms. Clinton, Ben Carson puts the massive federal debt at the center of his ideas about the nations direction. He specifically addresses the federal debt on his web page.

- He proposes a balanced budget amendment.
- National debt will destroy the future for the next generation.
- Lays responsibility for national debt on both Republican and Democrat parties.
- Says printing money to sustain the debt is irresponsible.
- Considers unfunded liabilities for social security and medicare as well as operating debt.
- Claims he would freeze the debt on his first day in office and force the government to live within its means.
- Would look at reducing the number of federal employees through attrition.
- Would force every government department and agency to cut their budgets by 3-4%.

Carson believes the debt is a threat to security and to the next generations:

"Our continued fiscal irresponsibility not only threatens the financial well-being of the next generation of Americans, it also increasingly jeopardizes U.S. security. Our international influence is weakened as our borrower status makes us vulnerable to threats from Mr. Putin and others. Perhaps worst of all, if our status as the world's reserve currency issuer changes, there could be a dramatic decline in our standard of living."

"If the government tried to pay that debt off by paying $10 million a day, 365 days a year, it would take 4,972 years."

http://www.nationalreview.com/article/222433/hillary-clinton-socialist-still-deroy-murdock

http://crfb.org/blogs/hillary-clinton-says-national-debt-real-national-security-threat

http://www.c-span.org/video/?c4548314/ben-carson-national-debt-fiscal-gap

http://www.cnsnews.com/blog/michael-w-chapman/mrs-ben-carson-if-we-pay-10-million-day-it-will-take-5000-years-pay-18

Marijuana Legalization and the "Drug War"

Hillary Clinton

At this point she hasn't come out for legalization of marijuana but has said that states can serve as laboratories to see how things work out. Clinton was quoted in a recent article:

"Earlier this year, during a town hall with CNN, she told Christiane Amanpour that she wants to "wait and see" how legalization goes in the states before making it a national decision. At the same event, she cast some doubt on medical marijuana by questioning the amount of research done into the issue.

Later in the year, Clinton labeled marijuana a "gateway drug" where there "can't be a total absence of law enforcement.'

"I'm a big believer in acquiring evidence, and I think we should see what kind of results we get, both from medical marijuana and from recreational marijuana, before we make any far-reaching conclusions," Clinton told KPCC in July. "We need more studies. We need more evidence. And then we can proceed.'

On her website, she suggests moving marijuana from a schedule I to schedule II substance which would allow study of its medicinal uses. Clinton is against selling the drug to minors and believes driving while under the influence should be illegal.

More generally, Hillary believes in reducing mandatory sentences for "nonviolent" drug offenses. She would turn federal law enforcement away from a focus on marijuana arrests to violent crime. She believes in increasing treatment rather than jail time for nonviolent drug offenders.

She has an emergency plan to attack drug addiction you can read here: https://www.hillaryclinton.com/issues/addiction/

Ben Carson

- Ben Carson is against legalization of marijuana.
- He supports allowing the use of marijuana for medical purposes.
- On the Glenn Beck radio program, Dr. Carson stated he would continue the war on drugs and intensify it.
- Carson has stated he views marijuana as a gateway drug.

He also stated:

"You know, we're gradually just removing all the barriers to hedonistic activity and you know, it's just, we're changing so rapidly to a different type of society and nobody is getting a chance to discuss it because, you know, it's taboo. It's politically incorrect. You're not supposed to talk about these things."

http://www.cnn.com/2014/10/16/politics/hillary-clinton-marijuana/

https://www.hillaryclinton.com/issues/criminal-justice-reform/

http://www.theatlantic.com/politics/archive/2015/10/ben-carson-intensify-the-war-on-drugs-and-keep-marijuana-illegal/411868/

Gay/LGBT Issues

Ben Carson is a deeply religious man so you won't be surprised he isn't as friendly to LGBT issues as Hillary Clinton. On her website Ms. Clinton touts her previous record supporting LGBT rights, including promotion of LGBT rights as human rights at the United Nations. She also reports that:

"updated the State Department's policy so that transgender individuals' passports reflect their true gender....That's why Hillary has spoken out against Republican efforts that would allow companies to discriminate against lesbian, gay, bisexual, and transgender Americans. Hillary also supports the Equality Act, which would mean full federal equality for LGBT Americans."

Carson states the following:

- He is in favor of civil unions for gay people.
- On gay marriage, he supports states rights. He supports an individual states right to sanction gay marriage or an individual states right to ban gay marriage within their own jurisdiction.
- He supports constitutional protections of human rights for gay people.

By supporting constitutional rights of gay people, you can infer that Carson is against discrimination against a person because they are LGBT.

https://www.hillaryclinton.com/issues/lgbt-equality/

https://www.facebook.com/realbencarson/posts/439171262916012

Veteran's Issues

After more than ten years of two wars, the United States has a lot of veterans, many suffering from the consequences of serious wounds and PTSD. Let's see how the candidates weigh in on support of veterans.

Hillary Clinton

Ms. Clinton declares unwavering support of veterans, with a mix of proposals to support veterans mixed with the usual liberal talking points. As with many of her writing many of her proposals are vague. Some of her thoughts on veterans include:

- She says she was "outraged" by the VA scandal.
- Against any privatization of VA healthcare.
- Will "demand accountability" from VA officials.
- The VA must provide health care "regardless of where people live".
- One of the few concrete proposals - she will expand treatment for substance abuse and mental health for veterans.
- She will increase housing support for veterans to end homelessness among veterans.
- Would expand programs for work training/education.

Ms. Clinton also engages in identity politics on this issue, stating:

"Women and LGBT veterans deserve equal recognition and equal support from their country. We must ensure the VA responsively serves women veterans, who represent the fastest growing segment of the veteran community. Also, we must recognize and honor LGBT veterans"

Ben Carson

Dr. Carson also sounds committed to veterans, but seeks to improve efficiency in the services available to veterans.

- Would move the Department of Veterans affairs into the Defense Department.
- Would transform VA health facilities from general hospitals to centers for specialized care such as traumatic brain injuries and limb replacement.
- Would provide veterans a health savings account that could be used at any medical facility in the country. This would include VA hospitals, DOD hospitals, or civilian hospitals.
- Proposes integrating a support system for service members that begins while they are in the military.

Like Clinton, some of Carson's proposals are vague and general without saying how he would accomplish them:

- Quickly process disability claims.
- Provide veterans with education and skills training
- Make specialized care for PTSD, traumatic brain injury, loss of limbs etc. readily available.
- Allow portability so the veteran can get healthcare in any location.
- Provide veterans with continuity of healthcare

Carson's proposals were incorrectly reported by many in the media as his desire to "eliminate" the VA, when in truth he proposed making it part of the Department of Defense.

https://www.hillaryclinton.com/issues/veterans/

http://www.cnsnews.com/news/article/melanie-hunter/ben-carson-we-dont-need-department-veterans-affairs

http://www.usatoday.com/story/opinion/2015/09/14/ben-carson-president-reform-veterans-administration-column/72219124/

Criminal Justice

Hillary Clinton's stances on criminal justice amount to criminal justice reform and gun control. Carson emphasizes cultural issues while agreeing that there is some police abuse. Overall, there is a surprising amount of agreement on some of these issues between the two candidates.

Hillary Clinton

Clinton's approach to crime and law enforcement is definitely liberal. She emphasizes police abuse, too much prison and excessive use of force. Increasing Federal influence on local police departments appears to be a big part of her agenda.

- "Invest" in "state of the art" law enforcement training that includes training on "implicit bias" and "excessive use of force".
- Double funding for the Depart of Justice Collaborative Reform program which provides "assistance and training" to local police departments implementing "reforms".
- Provide federal matching funds for police body cameras.
- Limit the transfer of military equipment to police departments.
- Create national "guidelines" for the use of force by police.
- Reduce mandatory sentences for nonviolent drug offenders.
- Retroactively apply the "fair sentencing act".
- Reduce the types of crimes that can be counted as a 'strike" in three strikes laws (another imposition of federal power into local laws).
- Increase discretion allowed to judges when applying sentences.
- End privatization of federal prisons.
- Treatment rather than prison for nonviolent drug offenders.

- Would take executive action to ban employers from inquiring if an applicant had a criminal record. This would apply to federal employers and contractors. She says this would give applicants with a criminal record "an opportunity to demonstrate their qualifications before being asked about their criminal records.".
- Restore voting rights for convicted felons.

Ben Carson

Ben Carson

- Police should have body cameras to help reduce police abuse.
- Acknowledges "driving while black" is a real phenomenon.
- Says he saw police abuses while living in Detroit but that personal responsibility is also an important issue. Emphasizes values taught or not taught in homes to many young men - no respect for authority, drug use etc.
- Has suggested foreign aid be diverted to inner cities in America to help alleviate poverty.
- Like Clinton, Carson supports restoring voting rights to felons once they have completed their prison sentences.
- Carson is against mandatory minimum sentences.
- Believes high out-of-wedlock birth rate contributes to crime.
- Emphasizes better communication is needed between communities and police.
- Says documented police brutality reflects "bad apples" and not police as a group or institution.
- Like Clinton, Carson has expressed concern over the large numbers of people in prison.
- Carson is against legalization of marijuana and believes the drug war should be intensified.
- Proposes "loser pays" to reduce lawsuits.

https://www.hillaryclinton.com/issues/criminal-justice-reform/

http://www.ontheissues.org/2016/Ben_Carson_Crime.htm

Education

Hillary Clinton

Like all Democrats, Hillary Clinton emphasizes education issues.

- Supports testing and reauthorization of No Child Left Behind act.
- Believes testing provides knowledge about how children "of color", students with disabilities and low-income students are doing compared to the general student population.
- Although she supports testing, believes we need to find the "right balance" of testing and standard instruction.
- Will "invest" in teachers and teacher recruitment. More training for teachers on "real world" learning experiences.
- Emphasizes students with disabilities.
- Supports universal pre-school. Wants every 4 year old child in the United States to have "high-quality" preschool.
- Supports Common Core.
- Opposes school choice and vouchers.

Ben Carson

Ben Carson is a strong believer in education, citing the role it played in transforming his own life. He believes that a better educated population will use less welfare. However he is against federal involvement in education.

- Against Common Core.
- Believes the public education system is a "propaganda system" for the left wing.
- Favors school choice and vouchers.
- Is against federal involvement in local school systems.

- Believes private schooling is better but public schooling could be improved by getting federal government out of it.
- Carson cites exams from previous eras to promote the idea our education system has been "dumbed down" and he believes we must significantly increase education standards.
- Carson believes like the founding fathers that the populace must be well educated.
- Carson believes education empowers people, and cites the example of slave owners not wanting slaves educated because it would have empowered the slaves.
- Runs his own scholarship fund for students that excel academically and demonstrate humanitarian qualities.

https://www.hillaryclinton.com/issues/k-12-education/

https://www.hillaryclinton.com/issues/early-childhood-education/

http://www.ontheissues.org/2016/Ben_Carson_Education.htm

Final Overview

Hillary Clinton

A Hillary Clinton presidency can be summed up in the following way. On domestic issues, Ms. Clinton will expand the role of the federal government, increase tax rates, increase the complexity of the tax code with more loopholes and credits for businesses and individuals, she will likely increase regulations both for the environmental and financial sectors. Ms. Clinton will act to reduce the number of people in prison (specifically for nonviolent drug offenses) and reduce mandatory sentencing. She will increase the involvement of the Justice Department in local policing in an effort to reduce police abuses. She opposes privatization of government activities at the VA and in the prison system. She supports Common Core. Hillary Clinton is against any changes to social security and in fact proposes more expansion of benefits.

Hillary Clinton has also proposed a large scale college affordability program. She also proposes government involvement or support for reducing a supposed epidemic of sexual assault on university campuses, LGBT rights, disability rights, and unions. She favors increased investment in infrastructure.

Other big Hillary programs include paid family leave, child care, increasing and the minimum wage. She also states she will work for 'equal pay" for women so would probably support passage of some kind of equal pay legislation.

Hillary Clinton favors keeping the Affordable Care Act or "Obamacare" in place. She also favors the "dream act" and a path to citizenship for illegal immigrants. She talks about a "strong border" but is not entirely clear on what that would mean. Her support of supposed "supervised release" of illegal immigrant families seems to indicate she would actually be weak when it comes to managing border crossings.

On Foreign policy, Hillary Clinton presents a more "hawkish" position than Barak Obama, but she says she will support the Iran Nuclear Deal. Clinton would probably sign or abide by a climate change treaty. While Clinton talks hawkish, she peppers her writing with a lot of rhetoric about "coalitions" and would appear to be very reluctant to commit U.S. ground troops to any military operation.

In Summary, its our view a Hillary Clinton presidency will be a continuation of the Barak Obama years, with increased government spending, programs, and involvement in daily lives of individuals and business. She will make the tax code more complex and raise rates on those deemed "wealthy".

Ben Carson

Ben Carson offers a direct contrast with Hillary Clinton, taking a solid conservative position on most issues. Unlike Hillary Clinton, Ben Carson puts the large size of the federal government and its national debt at the center of his view for the future direction of government. Dr. Carson believes that the national debt is a major threat to the future security of the United States and future generations. Therefore, under Dr. Carson one can expect a complete change in direction with either a freeze or decrease of budget for most government agencies.

On taxes, Dr. Carson is the complete opposite of Ms. Clinton. Rather than continuing with the current system and adding to its complexity with more tax credits and loopholes, Dr. Carson has proposed a flat tax of about 15% on all income including corporate taxes, while eliminating all tax credits and loopholes. It is Dr. Carson's belief that a simple tax system with lower rates will lead to an economic boom.

While he believes we should increase our use of "renewable" and other new energy sources, Dr. Carson does not favor large amounts of EPA regulation and would not sign any climate change treaty. Dr. Carson does not deny climate change is happening but appears to believe its mostly naturally caused and there isn't much we can do about it.

Carson is against marijuana legalization and believes we should increase our efforts in the "drug war". Carson also takes a harder line on illegal immigration. He does not favor deportation like Trump but is against a path to citizenship and believes in strong border security including fencing, drones, more border patrol agents and increased electronic surveillance. Carson would also get rid of sanctuary cities. However Carson has proposed a guest worker program at least for the agricultural sector.

Carson is against Obamacare, favoring private notions like health savings accounts instead. He is against common core and general involvement of the federal government in education. He is also against federal government involvement in local policing.

Carson has indicated a willingness to put U.S. ground troops in the middle east if it becomes necessary. He would probably be more "hawkish" than Hillary Clinton.

To conclude, in short Ben Carson and Hillary Clinton offer a very sharp contrast With Ben Carson there would be a complete reversal of direction with a smaller government and dramatic changes in the tax code and regulation. With Hillary Clinton it would be a continuation and even an expansion of the Barak Obama presidency. Of course both candidates face the problem of having to get their programs passed through Congress. If the Republicans maintain control of the Senate as well as the House, Ben Carson would have an easier time although its not clear the establishment Republicans in Congress would go along with his plans to completely revamp the tax code, for example - given that Congress is heavily influenced by lobbyists. So he might face an uphill fight.

With Hillary Clinton, if the Republicans maintain control of both houses of Congress she would probably have trouble enacting any of her bold plans. Its unclear how she will react to this, she might act like Barak Obama and resort to executive orders. She may be able to get small parts of her program passed, such as tax breaks for profit sharing or family leave. Our guess is that even if the Republicans control both houses of Congress many programs that conservatives don't favor will remain in place, including common core and Obamacare. If the Democrats were to win back the Senate, Clinton might be able to get more of her agenda passed